EVERYTHING YOU NEED TO KNOW
WHEN YOU'RE 8

Alan Dapré

'EVERYTHING
'you need to know,
'when you're,

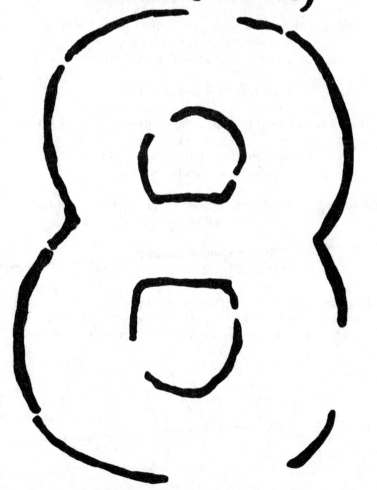

Piccadilly Press • London

Phototypeset from author's disk.

Printed and bound by Martin the Printers Ltd., Berwick on
Tweed
for the publishers, Piccadilly Press Ltd.,
5 Castle Road, London NW1 8PR

A catalogue record for this book is available from the British
Library

ISBN: 1 85340 340 7 (hardback)
1 85340 350 4 (trade paperback)

Alan Dapré lives in Nottingham, where he works as a primary
school teacher. He has written a number of plays, one of
which, *Kenny*, was chosen for Radio 4's Young Playwrights
Festival.

CONTENTS

INTRODUCTION

EVERYTHING YOU NEED TO KNOW ABOUT SCHOOL 1-62

INTRODUCTION

All grown-ups – believe it or not – have been eight years old. The trouble is they can't actually remember what it was like. Ask them and all you'll get is a glazed look. Show them a yellow, crinkly photograph of what they were like aged eight and they'll laugh at the embarrassing haircut and pretend it's someone else.

You see, adults go around acting as if they have been grown up all their lives, forgetting that somewhere in their distant, and very dim, pasts they were like you.

This book is for eight-year-olds everywhere who are worried they might end up like their parents!

Hard stare

Newspaper with big writing

Hairy ears

Embarrassing haircut

Beer belly

Worried look

Horrid collars

tissue

BEFORE YOU READ ON

This book is written just for eight-year-olds. If you are not eight – STOP READING – because these pages will self destruct in ten seconds ...

If you cannot remember how old you are (and this happens to all of us sometime or other) then try this quick test:

READ EACH QUESTION AND DECIDE
WHICH ANSWER IS BEST

1) *How many candles did you have on your last birthday cake?*
a) 0 – because Dad says he doesn't want me spreading germs when I blow them out
b) 8 – because I'm eight
c) ? – can't remember, but I had so many that I nearly burnt the house down.

2) *How long ago were you born?*
a) last week
b) eight years ago
c) when television wasn't invented.

3) *What is your favourite meal?*
a) mashed bananas and a soggy rusk
b) chips, chips and more chips
c) anything with bullet-hard sprouts and soggy cabbage.

4) *When you go shopping, do you*
a) get in the shopping trolley?
b) get bored?
c) get talking to the shop keeper about the price of boiled kippers?

What did you choose?

Mostly a's – Keep counting the birthdays.

Mostly b's – Congratulations! This book is for you. Read on, to find out everything you need to know when you're eight.

Mostly c's – Sorry, this isn't your pension book. You'll find it in the bottom drawer next to your false teeth and that itchy woolly jumper you like so much.

Good! Now we've got rid of everyone who shouldn't be reading this we can move on to the really interesting bits.

REMEMBER!

The following pages contain information
which is so secret you'll probably forget it the moment you move on to the next page.

Do not let this book get into enemy hands. It could land you in extremely hot water.

To keep this book (and yourself) in one piece why not read it:

1) wrapped up in a copy of the *Radio Times* (not you, the book!).

2) upside-down (not you, the book!).

3) at night, with the aid of special night-vision glasses.

HELPFUL HINT 1

● ●

If all else fails say you got it from Santa. There's not much anyone can do about that – especially if you say this in front of your baby brother!

● ●

EVERYTHING
YOU NEED TO KNOW
ABOUT SCHOOL

Have you noticed that grown-ups always drone on and on about *school* days being the best days of their lives? They talk warmly about cold school dinners, old teachers who are – sadly – no more, and the fact that it never used to rain on their Sports Days.

They are living in cloud-cuckoo-land. Life at school can be fun, but it can also be tough. There are a lot of lessons to be learned at school – both inside and outside the classroom.

WHAT IS SCHOOL ALL ABOUT?

At your age you should be used to school. Think about it. You have been going there for years. Some of you might remember spending some time in a Nursery – spilling wooden beads on the floor, and tipping sand down the teacher's back. Then you had a few years in the Infants – getting used to new words and old reading books. Now you are in the Junior department and you have to put up with long assemblies, hard maths and even harder chairs, held together with chewing gum.

1

So, you are probably thinking 'Why am I here?' Your parents will tell you that school is a very useful place. You get to do many things there that will actually help you. Not only will you learn how to write, solve maths problems, and read interesting books, you will also learn:

* How to add up money – which is great because you'll know how many crisp packets you can buy at breaktime.

* How to use an atlas – useful if you want to know where you'd like to go on holiday. You will, of course, end up at the place you went to last year, the year before, and the year before that!

Unfortunately, you will also learn a lot of useless things too.

* Teachers never go into the playground without a mug of lava-hot coffee.

* Kids always go into the playground without a coat, even in sub-zero temperatures.

* It is impossible to hang a school bag on your peg.

* No one ever claims the clothes in the Lost Property Box.

* School jumpers are always one size too big or too small.

Why not make your own list?

WHY GO TO SCHOOL?

●●●●●●●●●●●●●●●●●●●●●●●●●●●●●

There are three reasons why you have to go to school.

1) IT IS THE LAW.
It is your right to have an education. Since 1944 there have been several laws passed by the British government that set out in detail how children should be educated. Between the ages of five and 16 you have to go to school. There is no choice ... it is 12 years of hard labour!

2) IT GIVES YOUR PARENTS A BREAK.
Parents are a funny lot. One moment they are happily smoothing down your hair, covering you with soppy kisses, and telling everyone (Gran, Grandpa, next-door-neighbour, milkman) how wonderful you are.

The next moment they are rampaging, angrily, around the house like bears with incredibly sore heads. And all because someone (you) squeezed the tube of toothpaste in the middle, and forgot to wash behind the ears.

You see, little things like that drive parents crazy. So it really makes sense to get out of their hair and go and annoy someone else ... like a teacher.

3) IT GIVES TEACHERS SOMETHING TO DO.
Teachers come in all shapes and sizes, but they do have one thing in common. They are addicted to school. Okay, no teacher will actually come straight out and admit this but it is true.

Since the age of five (or possibly even earlier) your teacher has been going to school. Okay, he or she may have spent some time at college or university – learning to be a teacher – but that's pretty much like school, really.

Did you know that some teachers go back to teach at the schools they went to when they were kids!

In the same way that a snail cannot survive without its shell, a teacher cannot survive for long without a school. So, by going to school you keep teachers in a job and make them very happy.

WHEN YOU'VE SEEN ONE SCHOOL YOU'VE SEEN THEM ALL

ancient grease

● ●

A short history lesson ...
Children in Ancient Greece did a lot of the things in their schools that you do nowadays. For example, they had to learn an alphabet, practise handwriting

4

and read out their own stories. They were also taught to be good listeners and confident speakers. Well, actually, the boys were taught this. Girls wouldn't go to school: instead they would stay at home and – if they were lucky – might be taught how to read or write by a well-educated slave. (Possibly a teacher brought back in chains from another land.)

Boys in certain parts of Greece, for example if they lived in the city of Athens, would go to three schools. Each school would teach completely different subjects.

In one school the boys would be taught games and physical skills such as wrestling. In another, they would learn about the Arts, and take subjects such as poetry, music and drama. In the third school boys would read, write and practise their maths.

However, education in Sparta – another part of Greece – was quite a bit different.

Boys and girls in Sparta were taught many of the same things, including singing, athletics and dancing. They were treated as equals. At an early age, possibly as young as seven, boys had to leave their homes and move up into the mountains.

There, Spartan children would be taught how to live off the countryside, and shown how to fight using a variety of weapons. The Spartans were very keen to have a good army. So children in Sparta spent most of their time learning how to be skilful and brave warriors.

Life in Sparta was tough. Spartans are famous for not having luxuries. They did not appreciate good music or fine wines. They were not interested in the latest clothing fashions (eg, 'My chiton's* better than yours'), and had no time for good books.

GETTING READY FOR SCHOOL
● ●

Since you have to go to school you might as well go there ready for action. As an Infant you wouldn't have worried about getting ready for school. All the thinking would have been done by i) Mum, ii) Dad, iii) Childminder, or if you're really lucky, iv) Lady-in-waiting.

* long, woolly garment.

6

No doubt this kindly soul spent the early hours of the day packing your bag, getting out your clothes and preparing a packed lunch or breaktime snack. All you would have done is crawled out of bed, rolled into your clothes and made your way, bleary-eyed, to the school gates. Followed by a two-legged pack-horse carrying your coat, lunch, PE kit, wrestling figures, pencil case, rope, football and other everyday essentials.

Now you have left the Infants you are expected to be more responsible. This means that you now have to get ready for school by yourself. After all, you are eight!

So, what do *you* need to think about?

WHAT TO WEAR

Some schools insist that pupils put on a school uniform. This is usually a drab blue or grey and makes you virtually invisible when you're out in the school playground. Other schools allow their pupils to wear more casual clothing.

Typical school uniforms look like this:

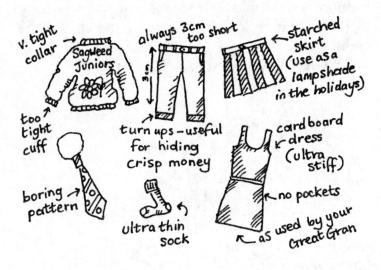

School uniforms have their good points and their bad points. First, the bad points:

1) Always itchy – even if you wear something underneath.

2) You look like everyone else.

3) The whole world knows what school you go to.

4) When you change back after PE you can never tell if you are wearing your clothes or your partner's.

5) It never fits.

And the good points?

1) You don't have to wear it in the holidays.

2) You value your other clothes more.

3) Everyone is dressed the same so no smart-alec is going to come over and tell you how cheap your top is (even if it is) as you can say the same back.

4) School clothes have this disturbing knack of lasting for years. You can spend ages running about like a wild thing and it still holds up. In fact you'll be worn out long before your uniform.

CASUAL CLOTHING
● ●

When schools let you wear casual clothes (eg, anything that isn't grey, black or dark blue) there is usually one rule to bear in mind: *Whatever you wear should be clean and smart!*

Look at these two boxes. One is full of acceptable clothing. The other is not. Can you guess which box is which?

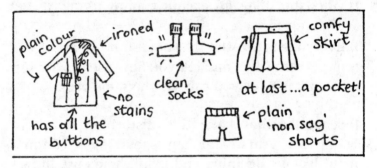

Wearing casual clothing to school does have its good points:

1) You are more individual. This means you can let a bit of your personality show through in the clothes you wear. If you like bright cheerful clothes then there is nothing to stop you wearing them.

2) You are probably better dressed than the teachers, who are still going around in clothes designed back in the 1930s.

3) No more of those nasty itchy trousers and razor sharp collars.

Bad points?

1) You spend hours each morning trying to get everything to match. Remember – 'Red and green should never be seen'. Or is it blue and green?

2) If all your favourite clothes are in the washing machine you might end up wearing something that is well out of fashion.

3) Instead of changing your clothing after school you probably have to wear the same clothes until you go to bed.

4) If you are in a school where some children have to wear a uniform and some do not then this might cause a bit of friction – even jealousy.

You should realise by now that all schools have their own rules about what you can and cannot wear. If you have to wear school uniform then try not to worry about it.

HELPFUL HINT 2

●●●●●●●●●●●●●●●●●●●●●●●●●●●●●●

Before you go to bed put out the clothes you will need the next day. Place them on a chair, or hang them up ready for the following morning. This way you will avoid a mad rush and you might earn yourself an extra five minutes in bed!

●●●●●●●●●●●●●●●●●●●●●●●●●●●●●●

WHAT TO TAKE TO SCHOOL

●●●●●●●●●●●●●●●●●●●●●●●●●●●●●●

Now comes the hard part – trying to remember all those things you need to make your school day run smoothly.

PACKED LUNCH

●●●●●●●●●●●●●●●●●●●●●●●●●●●●●●

No one knows what it is about school dinners that puts you off eating them. It could be the watery cabbage, the small helpings, or the simple fact that a lot of schools now have their meals bussed in from far-off places (like Siberia or the Arctic – they're that cold!).

Whatever the reason, school meals are on the decline (despite some fancy marketing gimmicks and poster campaigns). Some schools have stopped having them altogether and ask children to bring in a packed lunch – or go home for dinner.

If you still have a school dinner then don't worry. It won't kill you. School dinners are tested regularly by food inspectors, and all the plates and cutlery are washed ultra clean so they are sterile. That means they are completely free from germs. (It's just a pity the tables you eat off aren't anything like as clean!)

Right – back to the packed lunch!

There are two types of packed lunch that you can take to school.

The first is made for you and looks like this:

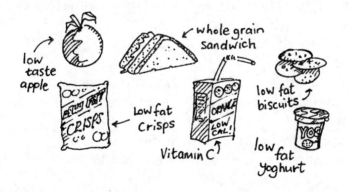

low taste apple

whole grain sandwich

low fat crisps

Vitamin C

low fat biscuits

low fat yoghurt

The second is made by you and looks like this:

fizzy drink

sugar sandwiches

CUSTARD CREAMS

lollipop

↖ high fat biscuits

↖ family pack of high fat crisps

Some people would say that the first type of lunch is much healthier for you. In truth, it doesn't matter which type of packed lunch you have as it's usually left on the back seat of the car anyway!

TASTY OR NASTY?
A class of eight-year-olds were asked to name eight 'terrifically tasty' treats and eight 'not so nice' nasties. Do you agree with what they said?

The eight tastiest foods are:

1) chips
2) ice-cream
3) turkey dinosaurs
4) pancakes
5) Yorkshire pudding
6) spaghetti bolognese
7) chocolate pudding
8) lasagne

The eight nastiest foods are:

1) sprouts
2) garden peas
3) cabbage
4) fried eggs
5) tongue
6) crab sticks
7) soup
8) liver

GAMES OR PE KIT

• •

You can always tell when it is a games day because no one in the class has brought their kit in. All the pegs in the cloakroom are 100 per cent bag free and the only person wearing trainers is the caretaker.

It is a mystery to teachers how a whole class can forget such a simple thing as a games kit. Every week, children all across the country fail to bring in their bags despite a million reminders by their class teachers the day before.

If a kit does happen to turn up at school it usually appears on a day when no games or PE lesson has been timetabled. The kit pokes feebly out of the top of a draw-string bag (made from Auntie Beryl's old pillowcase) and is left to hang sadly from the peg. Sometimes it rattles around in a shoulder bag the size of an aircraft hangar, or sits in wretched bundles on the cloakroom floor, gathering muddy footprints. Eventually it ends up in a plastic ice-cream tub labelled 'Lost Property!'.

If you really want to impress your teacher why not bring your kit in on the day you have games or PE? If you think you might forget why not write yourself a note and leave it on your bedroom door handle last thing at night, or tape it to your favourite packet of cereal?

Of course, if you are the only one who has brought in a kit there is more than a good chance that you still won't be doing games! No teacher is going to set up a whole lesson just for you. Instead, everyone will have to do that spelling test you've all been trying to get out of.

• •

It is a good idea to take your kit home on Friday night and bring it back into school the following Monday. Over the weekend you can make sure that it is cleaned (or mended) in readiness for the next lesson. There is nothing worse than climbing into damp, sweaty clothing that has been left in school for ages. Not only will you smell like a piece of mouldy cheddar, you'll probably look like one too!

• •

SOMETHING FOR THE MORNING BREAK

• •

It is very easy to wake up late and dash off to school with only a few mouthfuls of cold porridge to keep

16

you going. By the time you have had the register, done PE (ie gone to the cloakroom to see if you actually remembered to bring your kit), and survived an assembly it is breaktime. And of course, you're now ready to eat a vaulting horse.

It is really tempting to wolf down your packed lunch (or a friend's) but that then leaves you (or your friend) with nothing to eat at lunch time.

Why not make life easier and buy an alarm clock. That way you'll get up earlier and have time for a nice filling breakfast. Or – you could try taking a mid-morning snack.

A snack
(good idea)

A snake
(not so good)

There are two types of snack:
* Boring but rather good for you.
* Tasty but rather bad for you.

Look at this list of snacks. There is a tick by the ones that are good for you. All the rest should be eaten in small amounts since they contain a lot of sugar and/or fat.

celery stick ✓
cream cake
apple ✓
orange ✓
bar of chocolate
raw carrot ✓
pick 'n' mix sweets
crackers ✓
crisps
grapes ✓

Nine times out of ten you will get something boring but rather good for you to take to school. This is because your parents want to keep all the tasty snacks for themselves.

sounds like sour grapes to me

Most schools have a place where you can buy snacks. It is quite easy to find. Just look out for a long queue that snakes around half the playground. The snacks will be on sale at the beginning of this queue.

Joining this line does not always guarantee you the snack of your choice. By the time you reach the front the tasty goodies will have been snaffled up by the older kids.

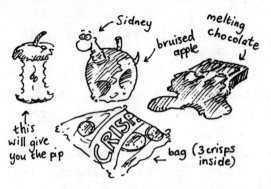

Sidney

bruised apple

melting chocolate

this will give you the pip

bag (3 crisps inside)

W A R N I N G !

●●●●●●●●●●●●●●●●●●●●●●●●●●●●

School snacks are always sold by the older kids (monitors). These older pupils are chosen for their trustworthiness, their honesty and their highly developed mathematical abilities. However – don't be fooled. They are highly trained mercenaries, with the counting skills of a broken calculator.

If you ever find yourself at the front of the queue – after a really long wait – be prepared for the following:

●●●●●●●●●●●●●●●●●●●●●●●●●●●●

1) A sign will go up saying 'No crisps left'. This is because the monitors have either eaten them all, or sold them to their friends first.

2) Your crisps will be the size of pencil shavings, because everyone before you has had a good feel of the packet. No one wants the unopened bag that contains three crisps!

3) Any chocolate on sale will be soft and squashy

because it is stored above the radiator in the secretary's office.

4) If there are apples on sale they will be covered in bruises, and the size of a dehydrated grape.

5) The whistle will go just as you are about to ask for something. The monitor will then smile and put the lid on the tub holding the money.

6) You realise your 20p is still in your coat pocket – and that you never wear your coat at breaktime.

OTHER THINGS YOU MIGHT HAVE TO TAKE

* Little brother or sister.

* Small toy to give the teachers something to confiscate and play with during their lunch hour.

* Football (plus coat and hat for goal posts).

* Skipping rope (useful for lassoing stray dogs and infants).

THINGS YOU SHOULD NOT TAKE

* Gran. She will start wandering around the

classroom looking for the desk she sat at when she was a little girl.

* TV. Poor reception, especially from your teacher.

* Favourite teddy. Might end up as a goal post or hostage.

* Your parents.

PARENTS AND SCHOOLS

Back in the olden days, before you were born, headteachers used to prowl along school corridors looking scary scowling at everyone, and teachers were only seen by mums and dads once a year at Parents' Evening.

Recently, things have started to change and these days, a lot of schools invite parents to come along to Sports Days, Book Fairs, School Plays, Carol Concerts and Sponsored Walks.

Some of these events raise money for the school, so you can have new maths books (!) and extra pencils to replace all those ones you keep losing.

Other events, like Parents' Evenings and Open Days, take place so your parents can find out how well you are doing at school.

THINGS YOUR MUM AND DAD WOULD LOVE YOUR TEACHER TO SAY

●●●●●●●●●●●●●●●●●●●●●●●●●●●

1) Butter doesn't melt in your mouth (or margarine).

2) You always put your hand up before talking, share sweets, and remember the Queen Mum's birthday.

3) You know your Times Tables, including tricky ones like 9 x 7 and 11 x 12.

4) You have a photographic memory.

whirr

hum

5) You have read all the books in the Juniors, and all the old newspapers in the art and craft area.

6) You can spell 'Supercalifragilisticexpialidocious'.

7) You can swim at least 25 metres. In fact, last week you swam the English Channel – twice.

AND THINGS PARENTS DON'T WANT TO HEAR

1) That you rush to the loo every five minutes.

2) That if all the pencils that you lost over the year were joined end to end they would stretch from Earth to Mars.

3) That your geography is so bad it takes you three hours to find your coat peg.

4) That you like school dinners better than the ones you get at home.

5) That you are always late for school. Next time you are late why not use one of these:

Eight totally original and never been used before excuses.

TEACHER: Why are you late for school?

YOU: (choose from these)

* My mum made me have a bath and I had to dry my hair.

* My sister borrowed my alarm clock and said she would wake me – but she didn't.

* I went to the doctor's for an appointment but the doctor was ill so I came to school instead.

* The budgie flew off with my socks so I had to find another pair.

PONGS AWAY!

* My dad's car broke down so I had to get a taxi and the driver got lost.

* I was so busy learning my spellings that I forgot the time.

* My dog followed me to school so I had to take him all the way back home.

*   I stopped to help the lollipop lady cross the road.

TEACHERS AND SCHOOLS

● ●

Think about the teachers you really like. Have you ever thought about what it is you like about them? A recent study showed that the best teachers:

* have a great sense of humour.

* praise you when you do good work.

* will help you if you have any problems with your school work.

* will talk to you if you feel worried about things at school. For instance, they will step in and stop you from being bullied.

* will be interested in the things you do outside school.

* are always ready to listen.

The best teachers are those you feel you can get on with. If your teacher makes you laugh, feel comfortable in class and eager to learn, then give three cheers and shout 'Hurrah' from the rooftops. You are well on the way to having a happy year at school with this person. When you feel good, your work will be good too.

Of course, you might be really unlucky and have a teacher who you don't get on with.

Some teachers are quite explosive and enjoy banging desks, whistling out of tune, and stomping around. A few can be eerily quiet, with a cold look that can turn you to stone.

What to do!
If you find yourself in a class where you don't hit it off with your teacher then the worst thing you can do is bottle your emotions up. Sooner or later you will explode. The best thing to do is find someone you can talk to. It may be your parents, a good friend, or perhaps another teacher.

Talking about the way you feel in class will make you feel a lot better all round. If it is hard to talk then why not get a pen and paper and jot your feelings down? Put into words all the frustrations and worries you have.

You do not have to show what you have written to anybody – just use the exercise to think about how you feel.

> *It's Great to be Eight because*:
> 'I get loads more pocket money and you get
> to join Cubs'   Matthew aged 8 and a bit

A QUICK SAFETY GUIDE: FIVE THINGS NEVER TO SAY TO YOUR TEACHER

● ●

1) *'It wasn't me.'* *
If you actually say this, 99.9 per cent of teachers will assume that you are guilty.

2) *'Is it breaktime yet?'*
Teachers have a knack of forgetting what time of day it is. Or even what day it is – that's why they write the date on the board first thing in the morning.

Even if a teacher is droning on for ages never be tempted to say that you could do with a break. If you do say this you certainly won't get one. Teachers are like that.

3) *'He did it first.'*
Teachers do not care about who did what when. They simply want to know why you had to get involved.

* Even worse if you say 'It wasn't me, it was Jim, Sue, Bill, Laura,' etc.

It's best to admit your part in what took place and let everyone else fend for themselves. That way, you won't have to hear the teacher say for the billionth time 'If he put his head in an oven would you be stupid enough to do it?'.

4) *'I forgot my kit'*.
Usually said in winter when you're trying to get out of a Games lesson. Another favourite is, 'I forgot my packed lunch'. Usually said when it is full of stale bread, and cold egg. Not a good thing to say since you might end up with a school dinner.

5) *'It's not fair.'*
Okay, so you were caught swinging on the toilet door and your friend wasn't. Now you have to miss three playtimes and your ex-best friend's outside laughing at you through the window.

It may not be fair, but it's life!

THE TIME AND THE PLACE
• •

Talking to your teacher is tricky since you have to remember there is a good time and a bad time for asking questions.

Sometimes you may find that your teacher is on another planet and isn't listening to a word you're saying. This usually happens when teachers are trying to write on the board in straight lines, or having to answer 14 questions at once.

It is a good time to ask questions when:

* half the kids in the class are away with chickenpox, measles, salmonella or Granny.

* the other children are quietly beavering away, and you can hear a pin/ruler/pencil/display drop.

* you are stuck, but you have really tried hard to think the problem through.

* your teacher is looking bored.

It is a bad time to ask questions when:

* you've just had a technology lesson where the only thing you made was noise.

* your teacher is scrubbing fluorescent paint off a brand new shirt or blouse.

29

* you have to shout over everyone else to be heard

* your teacher is arguing with the caretaker over whose job it is to take down the chairs

TEN THINGS TEACHERS ALWAYS SAY

Teachers spend most of their working lives saying the same things over and over again. See if you recognise these old chestnuts.

1) 'Who threw that?'

2) 'Put your pencils down.'

3) 'Be quiet at the back.'

4) 'I won't tell you again.'

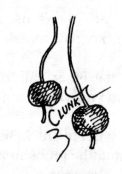

5) 'Stand behind your desks.'

6) 'Who forgot to wipe their feet?'

7) 'What did I just say?'

ANYONE KNOW WHY WE DON'T LEAN BACK ON OUR CHAIRS

8) 'Don't lean back on your chairs!'

9) 'Has anyone seen my register?'

10) 'If I've told you once, I must have told you a thousand times ...'

SPECIAL POWERS!!

●●●●●●●●●●●●●●●●●●●●●●●●●●●●●●

When teachers seem to perform amazing feats of mind reading and telepathy have you ever wondered 'How do they do that?'

It sounds crazy, but teachers claim to possess many special powers and abilities, including 'superhuman hearing', 'X-ray vision' and 'eyes in the back of the head'. Well, they would say this wouldn't they? But, exactly how true are these claims?

Case Study 1: EYES IN THE BACK OF THE HEAD

Picture the scene
While your teacher is looking out of the window you pass a note secretly to a friend, who is half hidden behind a lifesize model of the BFG (made of half-washed yoghurt pots).

Suddenly, the teacher leaps across the classroom and grabs the note from your friend's outstretched fingers. You both sit stunned while the teacher drones on about having 'eyes in the back of the head'.

The facts
Your teacher caught sight of your reflection in the window as you passed across the offending note. Waiting a moment (for maximum effect) your teacher then went into action. If teachers really did

have eyes in the back of their heads they would look like this.

HARD STARE

Remember: potatoes have trillions of eyes – not teachers!

Case Study 2: SUPERHUMAN HEARING

Picture the scene
It is song practice and you are at the back of the hall. You whisper to the person sitting next to you that you're not going to sing 'Morning has broken' ever again, since the only morning break you like is the one where you can buy crisps and run about the playground.

Suddenly, the teacher – who has been at the front by the piano – signals for you to get up. You stand and find yourself having to sing a dead embarrassing solo. Afterwards you sit, stunned, wondering if the teacher has 'superhuman hearing'.

The facts
You were unlucky. The teacher at the front of the Hall simply saw your lips moving and decided to teach you a lesson. No teachers have superhuman hearing because, let's face it, teachers can't hear themselves think in assembly, let alone anyone else.

PLAYTIMES
● ●

'Play' is the last thing children do during outdoor playtimes. No one feels like playing because playgrounds are so awful. You know the type – grimy rectangles of grit, surrounded by electrified fences and dead trees.

Typical playground activities include booting footballs at the dustbins, jumping in puddles, and falling off walls.

The only real excitement comes when the teacher on duty asks for a volunteer to take in the message that playtime is over.

In playgrounds up and down the country, small groups of bored children can be seen dodging flat footballs or wet skipping ropes. Others lean against graffiti covered walls, while the wind whips empty crisp packets out of their numb fingers.

Children hardly ever play games in school playgrounds. Boys usually wrestle each other to the ground for something to do, and girls just walk round in circles or jump over frayed strips of elastic.

School kids across the country were once asked whether they enjoyed being in the playground. The answer was a deafening NO! Perhaps this explains why most kids prefer to spend playtimes inside, running through school or hiding in the cloakrooms.

WET PLAYTIMES

There's nothing worse than sitting through an hour of handwriting practice only to see drops of rain dribble down the window just as playtime is about to begin.

Yes. It was sunny right up until the moment your teacher told the class to pack away, ready for break. Sadly, you look out to see dark clouds rolling menacingly in, lit by the odd flash of lightning. Thunder booms throughout the school, sounding just like chairs being put on the tables at home time.

The teacher dashes off to collect a cup of extra-strong coffee, leaving wobbly piles of scrunched up computer paper for you to draw on – as long as you use your own felt tips and *don't* touch the school ones. *Having* to stay in at playtimes is even worse than being in the playground!

PLAYGROUNDS

Schools shown on television quite often have cheerful outdoor nature areas full of newts, tadpoles and botanists, like David Bellamy. And there are always plenty of wooden seats dotted around so children (and the teachers) can rest those weary legs.

In short, playgrounds on TV are simply the stuff of dreams. Playgrounds in real life look like those vast tarmac runways at Heathrow Airport – worse luck.

A TYPICAL DREAM PLAYGROUND:

A TYPICAL NIGHTMARE PLAYGROUND:

(probably the one you've already got!)

After break it's back to THE THREE Rs

Unless you've been living on another planet for the past eight years you'll probably have heard grown-ups talk about 'the 3 Rs'.

A quick test.

Look at these words – can you spot The Three R s?

Resting	Writing	Relaxing	Reading
Arithmetic	Rollerskating	Rhubarb	Rambling

Time Up! The Three Rs are:

Reading, Writing and Arithmetic

All right, writing and arithmetic don't actually start with an 'R'. The point is that these words have 'R's in them. Complicated, huh? Well, that's 'basics' for you!

READING

● ●

Reading is a town in Berkshire. It is notable for its ancient buildings and ...
   (Wrong Reading, try again! – Ed.)
   Reading is a very important skill. (That's better – Ed.) For one thing, if you could not read you wouldn't have bought this brilliant book!

(What do you mean you didn't buy it?).

Watch out! Some parents treat reading like a race. Even before their children are out of nappies they're force-feeding them a diet of unappatising books and indigestible words. It's no surprise that these kids get a blockage and refuse to even look at a book when they are eight!

READING TIPS!

* Why not find a quiet place where you can sit or lie down without being disturbed. Feel free to sprawl over a few cushions. Put on some music and get yourself a drink. The secret is to make yourself nice and comfy.

* Join a local library. Not only will it have a large selection of good books, you will also find a lot of the latest ones. You could ask your family to join too, so that you can go there together. Come to think of it that's not always a good idea ...

* Always keep a pile of books in a handy place so you can browse through them whenever the mood takes you.

HELPFUL HINT 4

If you see a good book in a bookshop you can always ask your local library to order a copy. You can then take it out on loan. Some libraries make a small charge for this service, but it's still cheaper than paying for new books.

THINGS TO DO

* *

* Read a comic strip and cover the ending. See if you can guess what will happen next.

* Borrow a newspaper and pick out the front page headlines. These are the words written in thick black letters above a news story. Read the headline and try to guess what the story is about. The back page usually has the big sports headlines.

* Make a Reading Record each time you finish a book. Why not build up a collection of Reading Records to remind you of the books you have read? It could look something like this –

MY READING RECORD

Name of book:

Who wrote it?:

Illustrated by:

Date book was read:

What the book was about:

Who was in it?:

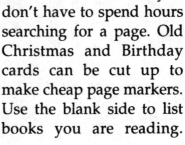

My favourite character:

The best part of the story was:

The worst part was:

Marks out of 10:

Your Reading Records will be more interesting than your dad's record collection.

*Make a bookmark so you don't have to spend hours searching for a page. Old Christmas and Birthday cards can be cut up to make cheap page markers. Use the blank side to list books you are reading.

41

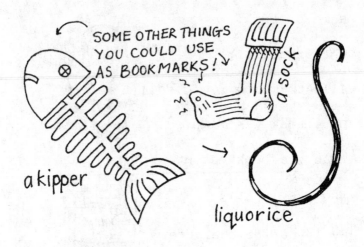

SOME OTHER THINGS YOU COULD USE AS BOOKMARKS!

a kipper

a sock

liquorice

In an ideal world, teachers would hear children read their reading books every day. In this idle world of ours, you will be lucky to get heard once a term. And even then the teacher will be ticking worksheets, stirring coffee, or chatting to the electrician (there's always at least one electrician in school pulling out the wires another electrician put in the day before).

Some people say that sitting in a bath full of ice cubes makes the hairs on the back of your neck stand up. The same thing happens when you read a brilliant book. Which would you rather do?

Imagine, you've read through a thrilling story. The action is hotting up. You are about to discover the fate of the book's hero when ... you get to –

THE LAST BUT ONE PAGE

David rushed through the stone opening and stumbled blindly down the worn staircase. He reached the heavy iron door and fumbled for the rusting key. He felt cold, dead metal beneath his fingers, and, not for the first time that night, the bitter chill of fear.

The key groaned as it twisted in the lock. David thrust his weight against the heavy door and fell forward gratefully on to soft wet grass. He didn't hear the low boom of the door as it closed, perhaps for good.

He fought to catch his breath, but the cold night air was thick, and stuck in his throat. Vast clouds rode the dark skies, choking the thin glow of moonlight. The figure in black had long faded into the gathering mist.

David knew his last chance was over and now they would come.. They would take his freedom and leave him nothing. It was then the howling began, and David knew he was about to ...

Yup! That was it. No prizes for guessing that the last page is missing. It's either lost or covered in yellow sticky tape or mouldy jam.

SILENT READING

Sometimes you will be asked to read by yourself. This is called silent reading but there's no such thing because all over the classroom you'll hear coughs, groans and rustly sweet wrappers.

PAIRED READING
● ●

You may be given a partner and asked to share a book. This is called paired reading.

Sharing an atlas or a reading book with a friend can be pretty cool. It means you can have a chat and plan what you're going to do at breaktime.

Of course, if the teacher's nearby then you'll actually have to start flicking over a few pages, but all in all it's not so bad, as long as your partner doesn't snatch your brilliant book and leave you with a dog-eared copy of Treasure Island written in 'ye olde boringe Englishe!'

WRITING
● ●

Look around and you will see writing everywhere; on crisp packets, rulers, washing machines, socks, rock, cans, CDs, shoes ... the list is endless. However, six thousand years ago there was no writing anywhere in the world. Someone had forgotten to invent it. So people up to that point in history had to remember everything (except their Ps and Qs, because there weren't any!).

Can you remember what you were doing this time last week?

Instead of writing things down, people would weave everyday events into stories, which they would tell to their children. Over the years, the stories would change a little because these storytellers might forget (or add) small details.

It is a bit like the game 'Chinese Whispers'.

Chinese Whispers

Sit in a circle with some friends. Think of a word and whisper it to the person next to you. That person passes it on. Make sure the whispered word goes right round the circle and back to you. The word you get back is unlikely to be the one you actually said.

THE FIRST WRITING
● ●

The first writing would have been done on a wall behind the bike-shed if schools had actually been invented at the time – instead it was done on little lumps of wet clay in a place called Sumer (near what is now called the Persian Gulf).

Pictures were drawn on to the clay using a bone, a piece of wood or a reed. Afterwards, the clay tablet
was left to dry in the sun or baked in an oven.

This picture writing was very useful because it meant the Sumerians could now remember important things like how many animals they owned or whose turn it was to do the washing up!

The Egyptians also developed their own style of picture writing. It is called Hieroglyphics, and they were used in Egypt for over 3000 years (until the Greeks invaded and told the Egyptians to use the Greek Alphabet instead!).

The alphabet you use today is based on the Greek Alphabet, but it was fiddled about with by the Romans. Not a lot of people know that.

46

Ancient picture writing tells us a lot about life long ago. We learn how people dressed, cooked – even what pets they had. The Egyptians, for example, were exceptionally fond of cats. It was against the law to kill them, even by accident, and when a cat died it was cat-astrophic news.

Before burial the Egyptians would wrap their cats up a bit like a bandaged finger.

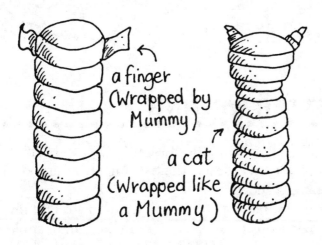

a finger (Wrapped by Mummy)

a cat (Wrapped like a Mummy)

WRITING AT SCHOOL

Whenever children stop writing they immediately begin fiddling with their pencils. No one knows why this happens, but at least five million pencils are tapped on table tops or dropped on floors *every single day!*

To prevent this happening many teachers expect their pupils to write non-stop from the moment they arrive to the time they leave. This has resulted in children suffering from dreadful ailments:

grooved finger   ski-jump nose

LETTER WRITING
●●●●●●●●●●●●●●●●●●●●●●●●●●●●

Writing letters can be almost as bad as a visit by the school torturer, sorry, dentist. Or an afternoon of triangle practice.

The trouble is you have to write in straight lines, be very neat and never make any speling misstaykes. Which usually means you do lots of rubbing out, or end up having to start all over again. (NB bad for the rainforests.)

If your parents find out you have learned how to write letters they will get you writing cringy 'Thank-you' letters after every birthday to horrid relatives who always send you expensive-looking parcels full of cheap jumpers and spotty hankies.

Looking on the bright side, if you know how to write a letter you can send one to Santa at the North Pole, and let him know you don't want another second-hand bike, especially as the last one looked suspiciously like the one your brother left rusting in the shed two years ago.

You can also ask Santa why the kid next door always gets better presents than you do.

Why not write fan letters to pop stars and famous footballers like Take That and Ryan Giggs? Or you could try writing to a pen-pal in another country.

POSTCARDS
●●●●●●●●●●●●●●●●●●●●●●●●●●●●●

Like letter writing, really. Except you have to remember to write smaller, and you don't have to write as much!

DIARIES
●●●●●●●●●●●●●●●●●●●●●●●●●●●●●

This is the sort of thing you write first thing Monday morning, while the teacher hunts for the plastic tub used to collect the Dinner Money. Diaries written in school tend to be about what you did at the weekend, or in the holidays.

My Weekend! ❁
On Saturday I went to my Grans and watched tele then I had some tea and Went home to bed. on Sunday I went to my Grans and watched ...to bed

Samuel Pepys was a famous diarist who lived in the 17th century. In his day there weren't any cheap flights to Tenerife or Florida so he used to fill his diary with home-grown stuff about The Plague or The Great Fire of London. Why not take a leaf out of his book and jot down who's away with chickenpox or what happened when the fire alarm went off.

COMPREHENSIONS

● ●

Very popular with teachers who hate kids. When you do them you are meant to answer the questions with incredibly long sentences that ramble on and on and on rather like this one. In fact, most kids write 'Yes', 'No' or 'Don't know' and spend the rest of the morning drawing a pretty picture underneath.

Here's one you might like to try. All you have to do is read the passage and answer the questions without falling asleep.

The Cow
A cow has four legs and lives in a field. It eats grass and produces full-fat milk. A lot of cows go 'moo'. Some star in pantomimes like Jack and the Beanstalk each Christmas. Most cows are called Daisy or Gertrude. They often have bells round their necks and horns.

Question 1) What has four legs and goes 'moo'?

Question 2) What do cows eat?

Question 3) Why do cows need bells
when they already have horns?

STORIES
● ●

These are great to do since you get to spend a
pleasant afternoon passing the rubber or
sharpening your pencil.

Okay, you may have to put pencil to paper
occasionally, but there are worse things you could
be doing.

Horror stories about school are very popular, and
usually have titles like 'Curse of the Dinner Ladies'

or 'The Haunted Lunch-Box.' Most suffer from frighteningly bad endings like, 'then I woke up and it was all a dream.'

Sometimes teachers get you to write dramatic true-life stories based on your own experiences. Anything from, 'Doing The Washing Up' to 'The day I Broke My Recorder.'

These stories always end with 'then I had tea and went to bed.'

Some children have a habit of writing THE END at the end of every piece of writing they do. It is a mystery why they do this since they never write THE START or THE MIDDLE.

HELPFUL HINT 5
● ●

Whenever you write a story go for a surprise twist where your readers are left gasping with amazement. For instance, you could have the hero of your story turn out to be an ultra-brainy criminal mastermind. Or a teacher!
● ●

INVITATIONS
● ●

These should be bright and cheerful. Whatever the occasion, try to make the words shout out – loud and clear!

Here are two invitations to a Birthday Party. Which one would you want to go to?

Dear Sue 🎁 🎈
Please come to my
BIRTHDAY PARTY on
Sun 20th at 3:00 p.m.
my house. ♪♫
We will have games, a
disco and a <u>magician</u>!
Name..........Date.....
yes I can/cannot come
to the party

Dear ~~Sam~~ Sue
I am having a
party and you can
come if you want
as long as you
bring a big 🎁
(your present
last year wos
rubbish!) Don't
wear nice stuff
cos I want to
look the best!

ARITHMETIC

The ancient Greeks were very interested in mathematics and loved solving complex brain-teasers. Many of their ideas are still in use today. A Greek called Archimedes enjoyed inventing crazy machines like catapults and water pumps, but he also had a reputation for being a dab hand at maths.

His best friend Hieron II, King of Syracuse (that's Sicily, folks), had a problem and Archimedes, a man of many principles, vowed to solve it.

ARCHIMEDES AND THE DODGY GOLDSMITH

One fine day (the weather's always good in Greece), a goldsmith made Hieron a splendid-looking gold crown. The King didn't trust the goldsmith so he asked Archimedes to find a way of checking whether the crown was pure gold – without, of course, leaving a scratch on it!

This problem gave Archimedes a real headache and he spent days racking his little grey cells for an answer. Finally, he put his feet up in a relaxing bath and was about to throw in the towel (pretty silly really – it'd get wet) when he noticed that his body had pushed soapy water up and over the sides of the bath. Archimedes suddenly realised this was the solution he had been looking for.

A dodgy crown will push up more water than a crown made of gold. Now – where's the soap?

He was so pleased with himself he leapt out of the bath and ran excitedly through the streets of Syracuse without a stitch on, shouting 'Eureka!' Which means 'I have discovered the answer!'

After a lot of crafty weighing and dunking with fake and real crowns Archimedes discovered that the goldsmith was pulling a fast one. Hieron II's crown was indeed full of cheap (base) metal.

Archimedes' actions in the bath spoke volumes – so the King had the dishonest goldsmith put to death for his crime.

Archimedes didn't fare much better. Years later, when he was an old man, he was stabbed to death while trying to work out another tricky maths problem!

Ancient Greece was not the only civilisation to use mathematics. The early Romans counted using a system of letters, and you can still see them in use on modern wristwatches and clocks.

Life today would be a very different without maths. For a start, no one would know how to use money, since you couldn't count it or share it out. Bridges would be worse than useless since you wouldn't be able to measure how long you should build them.

Sailors wouldn't know how far around the world they had sailed. And airline pilots would have no idea just how high up they were.

HERE, THERE AND EVERYWHERE!

●●●●●●●●●●●●●●●●●●●●●●●●●●●

Mathematics is all around you. When you pour
milk on to your breakfast cereal your brain is
working out the angle you should tip the bottle,
the distance the milk should fall, the volume of
milk needed to cover the cereal plus the time you
need to hold the bottle in the air. And you thought
you were only having some breakfast!

Just because you've had your cornflakes it doesn't
mean you have finished maths for the day. There's
plenty of it waiting for you back at school.
Usually lurking in dusty text books
full of addition, subtraction,
multiplication and
division problems –
set out like this:

16 plus 17   (6 + 4) x 3   Subtract 37
                                         from 51

Find the sum of 3 and 9

8 more than 9 =   Increase 6 by 14

38 x 2 = ☐

57

Teachers have a knack of slyly sneaking maths into your topic work too. In a topic such as 'Ourselves' you might have to find out your height and weight, or who is the tallest person in the class. This is topic work but it is still MATHS. And that means lots of running around with metre rulers and kilogram weights.

Did you know that a thousand fat bluebottle flies weigh the same as one kilogram? Unless a couple are on a low-calorie diet!

OTHER SUBJECTS IN SCHOOLS

HISTORY

Grown-ups are really impressed by historical facts. If you tell them the largest dinosaur was the Brachiosaurus (Bra key o saw rus) and it was the length of a full-size swimming pool they will think you are incredibly swotty.

GEOGRAPHY

Parents think geography in school is about discovering new horizons, and far off civilisations. In fact it's about getting the kids out through the nearest exit before the caretaker sweeps them up and deposits them into the boiler (along with rubbers, rulers and lost sixth formers on work-experience).

ART AND CRAFT

There are three reasons why you have to do art and craft:

1) so the teacher has an eyecatching display to put on the walls before the school governors look round.

OWCH

2) to get a cheap birthday present for Gran/Mum/Dad (usually a lump of squashed clay that won't stand up, and has a bit that keeps falling off).

3) because it is part of the National Curriculum and anyway it means Mum can dump all those unwanted yoghurt pots and clothing catalogues.

DRAMA

Nearly all of the drama in schools takes place in the playground. It has got to the stage where schools award OSCARS in the following categories:

BEST STUNT – nominations include:
– climbing on the roof to get a ball back

– falling off roof and landing on the school cat

MOST UNORIGINAL FIB – nominations include:
– the window was like that already, Miss
– I couldn't learn the spellings 'cos my dog ate them

BEST SENSE OF DIRECTION – nominations include:
– taking a message to the staffroom without ending up in the stock cupboard
– sending your teacher completely round the bend

BEST SUPPORTING PIGGY BACK

BEST SCORE (on a football pitch): 14 – nil

It's a fact!
Margaret O'Brien and Vincent Winter both won special film Oscars when they were eight years old.

PIECES OF EIGHT!
● ●

'Pieces of eight' is the favourite cry of pirate parrots, so we're told. A piece of eight was actually a large Spanish coin – it was worth eight smaller silver coins called 'reals'. This is really true!

Now read on for some more fantastic 'eight' facts:

* Your mum and dad would love you to be a musical genius like Wolfgang Amadeus Mozart –

who was so good at music he had written several symphonies by the age of eight.

* The ancient Romans used to call the number eight 'Octo'. It should give you a clue to the meaning of these words:

October – this used to be the eighth month of the year.

Octopus – an octopus has eighth legs.

Octogenarian – someone who has lived for eight decades.

Can you guess how many notes there are in a musical octave?

* Ross 154 is the eighth nearest star to the planet Earth

* Weight and height are both eight words – can you guess why?

* 'Gone with the Wind' won eight Oscars.

* HRH The Princess Royal is eighth in line to the throne.

* Coronation Street is the eighth longest running TV programme.

* An octagon has eight sides.

* The Jewish Festival of Light 'Chanukah' lasts for eight days.

* The ostrich is the world's largest bird and it is nearly eight feet (2.5 metres) tall.

* Great Britain is the eighth largest island in the world.

* Light takes about eight minutes to travel the 150,000,000 kilometres from the Sun to the Earth.

* You need eight rows of eight squares to make a chessboard.

* A snail takes about a minute to move eight centimetres.

* The number eight is 'otto' in Italian, 'huit' in French and 'acht' in German.

EVERYTHING YOU NEED TO KNOW ABOUT HOME

Home is the place where you go to after a hard day at school. Someone, who probably spent his life living out of a suitcase, once coined the phrase 'Home Sweet Home' – but there is nothing sweet about sharing your house with an evil-smelling brother or parents from the planet 'YOU-CAN'T-DO-THAT!'

Homes come in many styles:

semi-detached

detached or

very detached

Homes can also be terraced, which means you always have a pretty good idea what the people are doing next door. And because your neighbours are on both sides you often get it in stereo too!

People in France utter ze words 'chez nous' when they talk about where they live. Roughly translated it means 'our home'. Posh French restaurants with unpronounceable menus are sometimes named after the owners and called 'Chez Pierre' or 'Chez Gazza'.

As you race home from school you will go past houses with soppy names like 'Cliff Rise' or 'Buttercup Meadow'. Of course, you won't actually see any cliffs or meadows full of buttercups. This is called artistic licence.

There's always something happening at home. The washing machine sounds like a Space Shuttle on full throttle. Baby brothers throw tantrums and plastic bricks, and older sisters send earthquake tremors through the rafters as they do their step aerobics upstairs. The list – and the noise – goes on.

YOUR SPACE

Everyone needs a bit of peace and quiet now and then so it is nice to have a place that you can call your own – where you are not likely to be disturbed.

One room springs to mind – your bedroom. It may seem a bit small and feel freezing in winter (icicles hanging from the ceiling and all that), but the point is – it's yours! Tiddles has her cat basket, Rover has his dog kennel, and you have, well, your own bedroom. But you might have to share it! (If you do see page 73 for some life-saving survival tips).

What type of bedroom do you have?

TYPE 1
Peeling wallpaper first put up when your dad was a boy. The mattress on your bed sags so much you're halfway to Australia when you sleep on it.

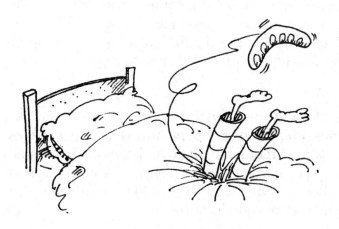

The windows are broken and whenever you try to stick a poster on the damp wall it curls up and falls off. When you try to get out, the door jams on the carpet and the door handle falls off!

Good points: you don't have to worry about your parents coming into your room because they wouldn't even if you paid them a million pounds. Mind you, if you had a million pounds you wouldn't be hanging around a dump like that, either.

Bad points: you have to sleep in it.

TYPE 2
Everything is shining like a new pin, even you. Your parents come in every day with a checklist and make sure that nothing has been broken, moved out of place, or breathed on. The colour of the wallpaper matches your eyes, and tones in nicely with the deep pile carpet (covered in plastic sheets so you don't leave any marks). The door is solid oak, opening and closing at the touch of a button. But of course you don't get to keep the controls.

Good points: there aren't any.

Bad points: you feel a bit like a dummy in a new shop window display. Welcome to a fun free zone.

TYPE 3
The drawers are bursting open with teddies, old games, and fuzzy jumpers. You can't move across the room without tripping over heaps of abandoned clothes, or piles of comics. Your bed was made, sort of, that morning and now looks more crumpled than Granny and Grandpa.

Your Thunderbirds wallpaper is still in good condition, and covered in posters of your favourite pop star. Unwashed mugs lurk beneath the bed, and spiders camp out on top of the wardrobe.

Good points: this room is much used and much loved. With a bit of thought it could be a great place to relax in.

Bad points: needs a good tidy up and clear out. And you won't get any help either!

If your bedroom is not really like the ones mentioned, don't worry. No two bedrooms are ever the same, but they will have some things in common like wardrobes, a bed, a lamp, a mess, etcetera.

WHY YOUR MUM AND DAD GIVE YOU A ROOM:

1) SO YOU DON'T HAVE TO SLEEP IN THE BATH
Sleeping in the bath is not a good idea. Not only will you feel a scary cold tap on your shoulder in the middle of the night, you'll have to share the bath with a hairy spider the size of a loo seat.

2) SO THEY CAN SEND YOU THERE WHEN YOU GET ON THEIR NERVES

Mums and dads are always sending their kids out of the way. If they could, they would put you in a cardboard box, take you down to the nearest post box and send you to the Antarctic.

Top five reasons for being sent to your room

i) walking over a brand new carpet in your muddy boots.

ii) 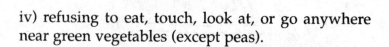 telling your baby brother to tip his banana custard over your grotty sister's homework.

iii) giving the greenhouse instant air-conditioning.

iv) refusing to eat, touch, look at, or go anywhere near green vegetables (except peas).

v) answering back.

● ●

Parents don't like it when you answer them back because, let's face it, you'll always say something a zillion times cleverer than anything they can think of.

However, the fact of the matter is that answering back doesn't get you anywhere – except sent to bed!

● ●

C) TO GIVE THEM SOMETHING TO WORRY ABOUT

Parents become miserable if they have nothing to worry about. As soon as a red bill drops through the letter box, or you hand over a dodgy school report, their eyes light up and they burst into life.

One of your parents' best worries is whether you are keeping your room neat and tidy. Of course, compared to worries like 'The Global Destruction Of The Rainforests' and 'Acid Rain' the state of your bedroom is hardly worth working up a sweat about. But that's parents for you. They will secretly keep an eye on your room and only need the flimsiest excuse to launch a sudden dawn raid armed with pump action air-fresheners, extra thick rubbish

sacks, and a turbo-charged vacuum cleaner.

Once your room has been tidied up your mum and dad will be more than happy to worry about something else, such as 'How long will it be before the bedroom is a tip again?" or 'Did we hoover up the cat?"

WHY DO PARENTS COME INTO YOUR ROOM?

There are several reasons why they do this:

1) TO MAKE YOU GO DOWNSTAIRS TO SPEAK TO YOUR RELATIVES
Some relatives love to stroke your hair, remark on how tall you've grown, and cover you with sloppy kisses. To save you this toe-curling embarrassment you should:

* wear a motorcycle helmet. Also put on a pair of flat-heeled shoes and your dad's baggiest jacket to make yourself look smaller.

* come downstairs covered in big red blotches waving a large, sticky hanky (use your mum's lipsticks and an old pillowcase dipped in green poster paint and glue). Roll your eyes, make your bottom lip tremble, and say miserably, 'I think I've caught a bug from school. The teacher says it's very contagious.'

Then sneeze a few times and wave the hanky about. Your relatives will be so afraid of catching something horrid they will make their excuses and catch the next bus home.

Don't boast about this to your brothers, sisters and friends otherwise your mum and dad might catch you out!

2) TO SAY THAT IT'S DINNER TIME
Meal times always happen just when you are in the middle of something interesting, like having a pillow fight or performing triple somersaults on the bed. They never happen when you are about to visit the dentist.

3) TO MOAN ABOUT THE FACT YOU HAVEN'T BEEN IN THE BATHROOM FOR A WHOLE WEEK
There is no point trying to explain to your parents that bathrooms are dangerous places. So show them the diagram on the next page instead:

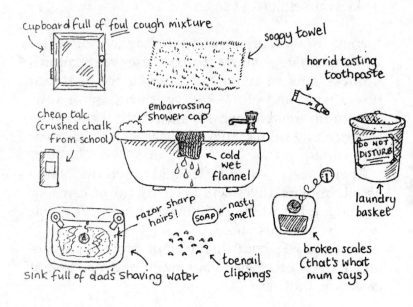

Cupboard full of foul cough mixture

soggy towel

horrid tasting toothpaste

cheap talc (crushed chalk from school)

embarrassing shower cap

cold wet flannel

DO NOT DISTURB

laundry basket

razor sharp hairs!

SOAP

nasty smell

toenail clippings

broken scales (that's what mum says)

sink full of dad's shaving water

4) TO SAY 'GOODNIGHT'
This is done in 3 stages.

Stage 1: Tucking you into bed so tightly you can't move.
Parents do this so you won't sneak downstairs and find them eating those tasty bars of milk chocolate that Granny bought just for you.

Stage 2: Reading you a bed-time story.
If you let your mum read she will keep stopping to ask you loads of tricky questions – just to check that you are listening. If you let your dad read he will fall

asleep at the most exciting bit and drop off the side of the bed.

Stage 3 : Turning off the light.
If the light is turned off you won't be able to carry on reading your comics or playing your brilliant computer games. So before your mum or dad leaves the room you should start sobbing into your pillow and crying a lot. (It helps if you stuff a piece of onion in your pillowcase first.) When the grown-up asks what is wrong say that you are afraid of the dark. With luck, you should have a light left on ALL NIGHT!

SHARING A ROOM
● ●

Sharing a bedroom is like climbing Mount Everest while wearing rollerskates on the wrong feet. In other words, it is a challenge. No eight-year-old wants to be shut up with a brother who leaves smelly socks everywhere, or a sister who snores. The trouble is, there isn't much you can do about it. Unless you go and live in the shed.

Sometimes you will feel like getting out a tin of paint and slapping a thick white line across the floor. This is not a good idea because the other person will deliberately walk over the line and leave splodgy footprints on your bit of the carpet!

Sticking huge signs on your side saying 'KEEP OUT!' or 'BEWARE, KILLER TEDDY!' might make you feel better, but that won't work either. It is more likely just to cause another row.

● ●

When you first share a room, and if you haven't always shared one, you will have a lot of rows, but many of these can be avoided if you sit down with your sibling (brother/sister) and sort out some basic rules. These rules page should help start you off.

● ●

Rule 1: Get into the habit of tidying the room up as you go along.

When you finish with a game or a book it only takes a moment or two to put it away. If you leave a heap of things out you won't find anything when you want it. And someone might accidentally tread on them.

Rule 2: Try to keep junk off your tables and drawers.

Rooms look much neater when surfaces are cleared of mess. Jars of make-up and bottles of perfume soon get in the way, and can easily be knocked over – making more mess! Store fiddly things like rings and chains in small boxes, which you can put away in a drawer. You can buy jewellery boxes but it is cheaper to use a plastic margarine tub: glue a piece of foam inside the bottom of the tub (this will stop your rings from getting scratched), and then cover the outside with gold paint or coloured paper.

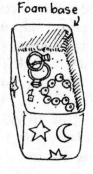

Foam base

Rule 3: Keep track of your possessions.

The secret here is to stop your things from wandering around the room. How many times, for instance, have you gone looking for a jumper only to find *it is not where you thought you had left it*?

Make life easier by storing your things in boxes. You can then stick on labels saying what is inside.

USEFUL STORAGE BOXES

Fill this with musical instruments, squeaky toys and noisy computer games

Fill this with cuddly toys, plastic figures and bulky toys

Fill this with a cricket bat and stumps, frisbees and skipping ropes

Fill this with board games, packs of cards and colouring pads

Fill this with drawing paper, modelling clay, lego, *(keep a small tub in the box and put in sticks of glue, a stapler, scissors, needle and thread)*

Fill this with books, paints, comics, interesting newspaper clippings

Why not have a BITS 'N' PIECES box so you can put in half finished drawings, old school work, conkers ... ? This can be sorted out on a rainy day or whenever you feel like it.

Storage boxes can be bought quite cheaply from DIY stores, and also from many supermarkets and toy shops. A cheaper alternative is to collect some strong cardboard boxes when you next go into a large supermarket. They are usually piled up by the checkout tills. Fill a couple with shopping and bring them home. Then give them a wipe, paint them bright colours and glue on a large label!

Some shops have cardboard crates (that once held tomatoes and fresh veg) which are ideal to fill up and slip under the bed.

Rule 4 : *Make the best of it.*

Sharing is not easy. There will be times when you feel like screaming, especially if your brother has the television on when you want to get to sleep, or your sister won't stop singing out of tune. Remember that there will be good moments too. Swopping secrets late at night, or sharing a midnight snack is something only you can do. So, look on the bright side. When you're feeling lonely there will always be someone nearby to turn to – even if they do have smelly feet!

And you can always throw a few rotten jokes at each other!

Eight Best Worst Jokes

* What do you call a sick alligator?
An illigator!

* What is Winnie-the-Pooh's middle name?
The

* What do you get if you cross a mole with a hedgehog?
Tunnels that leak!

* Why did the pig cross the road?
Because it was the chicken's day off.

* What did one wall say to the other?
I'll meet you round the corner.

* What does an electric eel taste like?
Shocking!

* How do teddy bears start their races?
Ready ,Teddy, Go!

* What did the sea say to the sand?
Nothing. It just waved.

YOUR FAMILY
● ●
DAD
● ●

Other names: Daddy, Dada, Papa, Pa, Pater, Father, Popsy wopsy

Dads may look different from each other but they do have quite a few things in common. For instance, dads like you to laugh at their weedy jokes, they expect second helpings of pudding (while you get none), and they love their cars more than anything else in the world – including you!

Dads are famous for having lots of bad habits, for instance they:

* change over to a
different TV programme
without asking anyone
else.

78

* eat with their mouths wide open and tell you off if you do it.

* cheat when you play a game, especially if you're about to win.

* always make you go in goal!

A dad also wears odd socks, gets you to clean his car (for a measly 20p), hogs your computer games, and always wants the last word!

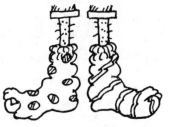

Dads can be quite useful if you ever have a puncture on your bike tyre, or you need to know how to cook beans on toast. They are no good if you need splinters taken out (because they go white as a sheet and fall flat on their faces) and they are rotten at driving (even if they do think they are ten times better than Damon Hill).

MUM
● ●

Other names: Mummy, Mama, Mam, Mom, Ma, Mater, Mother, Mumsy Wumsy

Mums are brilliant at organising things (eg trips, Dad, you). They are usually very patient and loving but it is possible to push them too far!

Mums have fantastic memories and remember important dates like birthdays and Christmas – Hurrah! Unfortunately, they also know down to the nearest millisecond when you're next due at the dentist, and when it's time for a haircut.

Your mum also always knows what you are thinking:

There are some things you do that drive your mum crazy. Such as:

1) climbing into the supermarket trolley while she is pushing it – when it is already overflowing with shopping

2) saying the same thing over and over again

3) sitting down at the dinner table without washing your hands

4) fiddling with your nose

But what about their habits? Have you noticed how Mums are famous for:

* asking you questions you can't answer:
– 'What am I going to do with you?'
– 'When will you ever learn?'
– 'Why do I waste my breath?'
– 'Who do you think you are?'

What did I just say?

* saying 'Just one more mouthful' and then making you eat another fifty

* stopping to answer the phone, even if you're already halfway down the street, and very late for karate!

* picking at their food   * picking at your food

   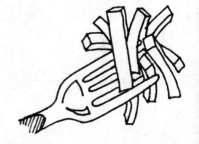

Your mum will also think that YOU are never as well-behaved as the friends you bring round to play. Even if you tell her that this is what their mums say about you!

LITTLE BROTHER

Barmiest behaviour: Hangs around outside your bedroom door all day hoping you will play games with him. Does this even when you are out!

Horrible habit 1: Embarrasses you in front of your friends by saying Mum still combs your hair (and cuts it with the kitchen scissors).

Horrible habit 2: Tells tales and runs to Mum even if a) you haven't done anything wrong and b) his shoes are on the wrong feet.

Sneakiest trick: Can squeeze out huge crocodile tears.

Good points about little brothers:
* You always have someone to talk to when none of your buddies can come out to play.
* You can jump on them for no reason.

LITTLE SISTER ●●●●●●●●●●●●●●●●●●●●●●●●●

Barmiest behaviour: Will try and talk to you when you are asleep!

Horrible habit 1: Will take your toys and a) break them into little pieces or b) leave some lying about so Dad trips over them – and blames you.

Horrible habit 2: Hugs you when she's covered in sticky chocolate and other things too disgusting to mention since this is a family book.

Sneakiest trick: Can look really cute so she gets all the attention at weddings and birthday parties.

Good points about little sisters:
* They say nice things when you need cheering up.
* They won't go around karate kicking and wrestling your teddies.

BIG BROTHER
● ●

Barmiest behaviour: Will be horrible to you at home but protect you from bullies at school.

Horrible habit 1: Sticks your favourite toys on top of a wardrobe so you can't get them.

Horrible habit 2: Loves to tease you about the fact he can stay up an hour later than you.

Horrible habit 3: Will jump on you for no reason.

Sneakiest trick: Never admits to doing anything wrong and always manages to get the blame on you.

Good points about big brothers:
* They might help you with your homework.
* You can play games with them, as long as you let them win!

BIG SISTER

MUM – HE'S RUINING MY TIGHTS AGAIN

THE BOY IN THE NYLON MASK!

Barmiest behaviour: Spends hours every week buying new clothes and then complains that she never has anything decent to wear!

Horrible habit 1: Spends more time in the bathroom than any other room in the house.

Horrible habit 2: Leaves her clothes all over the house.

Horrible habit 3: Puts dirty plates down on the floor so you tread on them.

Sneakiest trick: Always goes into the bathroom just when you want to!

Good points about big sisters:
* They will bribe you to keep quiet when they bring their boyfriends round.

HAPPY FAMILIES?

● ●

The families you see in television adverts never row, never leave their wet socks on the radiator and never stop being perfect. They love eating frozen meals which look massive on TV but are very small in real life. These TV families have pure white teeth, drive about in really clean cars, and always wash their clothes in two brands of soap powder.

Spot the Difference!

A TV family

A TV watching family

In real life you won't sit like a little angel at the table waiting patiently for your very small gristle burger. No, you'll be turning your nose up at everything on the plate and making a grab for the biscuit tin, while your sister spills flat cola over the tablecloth.

Mums and dads may sometimes decide that it is best if they divorce (live apart).This means that their kids have to get used to a different type of family life. Which is not always easy.

These boys and girls may even blame themselves for the split between Mum and Dad. They can think that it is all their fault and become very unhappy. This may affect their appetite or school work. It is hard for them to see that they have done nothing wrong.

If you have friends who are upset because of what is happening at home, ask them if they want to talk about it. Talking is good because it helps us let out our feelings of anger or sadness.

No families are always 100 per cent happy. There will be days when your family drives you bonkers. You may, for instance, feel like bopping your brother over the head with his annoying squeaky teddy.

But, don't forget that there will be days when you drive everyone else round the bend. Mum may get miffed because you haven't tidied up your room properly, and Dad may be upset because you dropped your dinner over his favourite Garfield slippers!

This is all part of family life and there is not a family in the world (except on TV) that doesn't have the occasional fireworks.

THE FAMILY PET
● ●

Pets are lovely to have around the home. Fascinating to watch, they can also be nice to cuddle and fun to be with. And the great thing is you can always find a pet to suit the home you live in. Mind you, there are so many pets to choose from, you could be nine before you get round to picking the one you want!

'I want a rabbit because it is soft.'   Jenny aged 8

'I want a sweet cute baby lion that will never grow up.'   Trudy aged 8

'A kitten because I can play with it. all day and take it for walks.'   Rhiannon aged 7

'I would love a snake so I can feel it.'   Ben aged 8

'Tarantulas. They are nice and furry.'   Tim aged 8

EIGHT GREAT REASONS TO OWN A PET
● ●

1) Pets never tell you off.

2) They can help keep you fit.

3) They like having you around.

4) Pets won't sulk if you forget to invite them to your birthday party.

5) They never bully.

6) They don't tell you to do your homework.

7) They are great to talk to.

8) Pets don't care what you look like.

Since even small animals can be a big responsibility it's a good idea to ask if you can have a pet before you bring one home.

Pet checklist
Your pet will need:

* Clean water
* Shelter
* Exercise
* The right food
* Lots of love

Gerbils, parrots, mice, rats, budgies and canaries are often picked as pets but, since they are hopeless at shopping and can't use the tin opener, they will need lots of care and attention.

PRACTICAL PETS
● ●

Dogs are the most popular pets in Britain, which means a lot of eight-year-olds are barking mad about them. It's not difficult to see why. Dogs are playful, affectionate, and love lots of fuss. They also love jumping in puddles, running round in circles and chasing toilet rolls.

Fish are very practical pets because they don't take up much room, never chew your slippers and you won't have to keep taking them for walks. Some have quite bubbly personalities.

Cats make good pets because they are clean, friendly and independent. Most cats sleep for about 16 hours a day, and then disappear just when you want to play with them or take them to the vets. Cats always want to be let back in two seconds after they go out, and love leaving muddy footprints all over your homework/bed/gran.

Hamsters like shredding paper so they are great for getting rid of dodgy school reports and unwanted Valentine cards.

HELPFUL HINT 8
● ●

Pets don't have to be expensive. In fact a lot of pets won't cost you anything since you can find worms, insects and spiders in the garden, usually under large stones. Slugs and snails are very easy to spot because they leave a slimy trail behind them, a bit like baby brothers.
● ●

If you don't fancy a pet animal why not try a pet rock, a pet sponge or a pet shoelace?

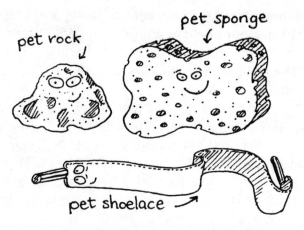

pet rock

pet sponge

pet shoelace

They're house-trained, unusual and don't need a lot of looking after. Of course, you'll still need to give this strange pet a name and lots of fuss – just as you would any pet.

Or why not fool your friends with this pet-tastic idea! *

STICK INSECT (twigus twigus)
● ●

What you need:
* glass jar with holes in the lid
* a few leaves
* handful of soil
* packet of twiglets

Instructions:

1) Open the packet.

* Guaranteed not to smell, bite, scratch or leave puddles on the carpet.

2) Take out a twiglet and scoff
the rest while no one's looking.

3) Put the soil and the leaves
inside the jar.

4) Drop in the twiglet.

5) Screw on the lid.

PET ALIENS

These pets are really and truly 'out of this world'. Of course, grown-ups will tell you that aliens don't exist, but this is just a cunning plot to stop you from having one.

If you look out of your bedroom window at night you will see trillions of shiny stars and planets.

They shine so brightly because a lot of aliens are scared of the dark and like to leave a light on when they go to bed.

Aliens make great pets because:

* they can do your homework in half the time (since two heads are better than one!).

* you get to go to school in a supersonic spaceship instead of a clapped out school bus.

* if you break a saucer while washing up, they've always got a spare one.

Some aliens:

* pick their nose every morning.

* have funny names like 'blibble' or 'frptlppt'. (Mind you, they think your name is much funnier.)

* earn extra pocket money starring in episodes of 'Star Trek' and 'Dr Who'.

* don't believe humans exist.

EVERYTHING
YOU NEED TO KNOW ABOUT FRIENDS AND FREE TIME

FRIENDS

A friend is someone who you get on well with and can trust. A good friend:
– cheers you up when you feel sad.
– shares things with you.
– says nice things about you.
– is pleased to see you.
– listens to the things you have to say.
– is interested in your hobbies and perhaps likes some of the things you like, eg holidays and cream cakes.

MAKING FRIENDS

It can be a bit scary making new friends, because you usually have to go up and talk to someone you don't know. If you are quite shy a good way to meet other eight-year-olds is to join a club. The chances are you will make new friends and have a load of fun too.

96

If you enjoy going for a swim you could join a local swimming club. Because everyone there has the same hobby you'll soon get chatting away.

Your Yellow Pages, or the local leisure centre should be able to give you a list of clubs that eight-year-olds can join. You could try one of these activities:

walking   swimming   cycling   golf   bowling
badminton   squash   tennis   dance classes
martial arts classes   judo classes   exercise classes
movement classes

Or you could always have a go at one of these eight terrific team games:

football   rugby   netball   cricket   hockey
rounders   basketball   volleyball

Swimming goggles
American Football helmet
Jacket (for Martial Arts)
Canoeing life jacket
Judo belt
Hockey stick
Cycling shorts
Cricket glove
Football boot
shin pad
ice skate

Getting friends can be a bit of a worry. But so can keeping them.

Worry 1: That you haven't got the latest trendy trainers or clothes.
Make your friends notice you not your clothes. If you show them you are a good listener and a caring friend you will soon find they are not bothered about what you are wearing, or how much it cost.

Worry 2: That your friends will go and play with someone else.
We often lose friends if we show off or are too bossy. Sometimes we lose them if we argue too much or keep cracking the same rotten jokes. A good tip is to think about what you are going to say or do before you say or do it.

Worry 3: That a friend might talk about you behind your back.
If this happens then it's probably best to stay cool and choose a new friend who you feel you can really trust. Why not get to know some of the quieter kids in the class (or on your street). They're probably a lot friendlier and nicer anyway.

INVITING FRIENDS ROUND

Asking friends round to your house to play is a great idea because it means:

1) sausage, chips and beans for tea.

2) your brother will go out in a sulk because his friends aren't coming.

3) you won't have to do the washing up.

4) Mum gets out the choccy biscuits.

HELPFUL HINT 9

Before they arrive make sure you have cleared a space to sit down in your bedroom and Gran has picked up her false teeth (leg, eyeball, etc). And check your brother hasn't put a squished spider or piece of week-old chewing gum under the biscuit tin.

You will find lots of fab games you can play with your friends beginning on page 113.

LETTING YOUR BEST FRIEND STAY OVER
•••••••••••••••••••••••••••••••

If you promise to do loads of homework and wash the car every Sunday for the next week/month/year your mum and dad will probably let your best friend stay over. To make the night really special why not:

* sneak a few packets of crisps, some biscuits and other yummy snacks upstairs. Set an alarm clock for twelve o'clock and put it under your pillow (so it doesn't wake the whole house up) and have a midnight feast.

* get a few spooky stories from the library and scare each other to sleep

* play some quiet board games when it gets dark using a torch to see what you are doing. (Watch out there's no cheating!)

* make shadow pictures on the wall by moving your hands in front of a torch or a small spot lamp.

* sit by the window when it is dark and watch scary tree branches sway in the night. You might be very lucky and see nocturnal animals like hedgehogs, foxes and badgers rummaging about for food.

STAYING AT A FRIEND'S HOUSE

Mums and dads will be only too pleased to let you stay the night at a friend's house. They agree, not out of the goodness of their hearts but because they know they'll have lots of lovely peace and quiet once you've gone.

Before you go to your friend's you will need to pack an overnight bag. Not sure what to take? Here are eight extra-essentials:

1) teddy to protect you in case you have to nip off to the loo in the middle of the night.

2) pyjamas – not the fluffy nylon ones but the cool ninja kick-boxing ones.

3) toothbrush to protect your teeth from plaque, tooth decay and hairy spiders in the sink.

4) Computer game – one that has its own light for nocturnal use.

5) clean socks, undies, etc.

6) comics and torch.

7) alarm clock.

8) secret snacks.

FREE TIME

•••••••••••••••••••••••••••••••

THINGS TO DO WITH YOUR FAMILY

•••••••••••••••••••••••••••••••

'The family that plays together stays together' is one of those old sayings that your granny or teacher are fond of. Like many old sayings there is probably some truth in it.

Doing things as a family such as going on walks together and playing games together gives the family a chance to talk and enjoy Dad's bad jokes. In this section you will find suggestions for things you can do with your family, and by yourself when you have some Free Time.

* Open a map of your local area and go to a place no one has been before. It might be a trip to a park or nature reserve. You might visit a crumbling historical mon- ument (no, not school), an art gallery or a local museum. Take a sketch pad and some pencil cray- ons with you to a gallery and have a go at copying some pictures.

* Challenge your mum and dad to a drawing competition. Sit in front of a Still Life (a group of objects, eg a bowl of fruit, a vase of flowers, even a toaster!) and get everyone to draw it – without looking at the paper.

* Sort out your room and collect up things you don't want any more, and any clothes you have grown out of. Make posters and invitations asking neighbours and friends to come along to a Bring and Buy stall in your garden (or garage). Ask the rest of your family if they have anything to donate. Put on refreshments like tea, coffee and squash as an extra attraction. Any money raised can go to charity.

* Grans and grandads are a great source for photos of your mum and dad when they were young – especially those really embarrassing ones! Collect the snaps in an album, along with some stories that the wrinklies have told you, and – hey presto – you have a really great Christmas present.

* Spend a quiet Sunday afternoon at the local swimming pool practising your front and back strokes. If your parents can't swim why not have a go at teaching them?

GAMES TO PLAY WITH YOUR FAMILY
● ●
* Put on a blindfold and ask someone in your family to take you on a walk through a place you know

really well. It could be the garden, the local park or even upstairs. Start by holding hands and when you feel more confident let yourself be directed by your partner's spoken instructions.

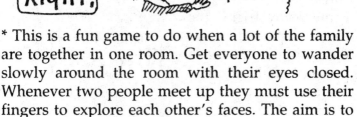

* This is a fun game to do when a lot of the family are together in one room. Get everyone to wander slowly around the room with their eyes closed. Whenever two people meet up they must use their fingers to explore each other's faces. The aim is to guess who the other person is.

* Put a list of things on a tray, eg marbles, cards coins and fruit. Ask your family to study everything on the tray very closely for 30 seconds. Then cover the objects up and see if everyone can remember all the objects.

You can also play a slightly different version where you take one thing away and your family has to guess what the object was.

* Split the family into pairs. Each pair must stand face to face. Get one person to mime an action for the other person to copy. For the mimer it should be just like looking in a mirror.

* You will need a large piece of newspaper. Ask someone to choose an object or animal. The aim of the game is to tear the paper into the shape of the thing chosen. To make the game really tricky, the paper is passed round the group and each person is only allowed one tear.

a pig

and its litter

* Pass the smile. Everyone sits looking miserable. Start the game by wiping the smile off your face (with the palm of your hand) and throwing it at someone else. That person has to grab the smile and put it on. Then it is wiped off and thrown at someone else.

THINGS TO DO IF YOU ARE BY YOURSELF

* Go to Mum or Dad and offer to do any jobs round the house which they hate doing – for a small fee. If they agree you will have some extra pocket money and they will have a boring job out of the way. (Try weeding, cleaning out the pet's cage, washing the car, etc.)

●●●●●●●●●●●●●●●●●●●●●●●●●●●●●●

STOP PRESS!

All you need to know about pocket money!

* Pocket money should *never* be put into your pocket because pockets have holes and *holes = no money* (see Pic. 1)

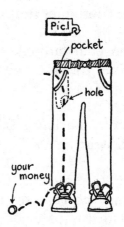

* Always keep your money in a safe place e.g. around your waist (see Pic. 2) or in a SHP (Secret Hiding Place) *away from brothers, sisters and parents*!

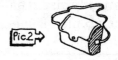

* Yes, many eight-year-olds know to their cost that mums and dads give them pocket money and *then ask for it back*! *

inside a boring book

inside an old trainer

inside an old cuddly toy

| SHP 1 | SHP 2 | SHP 3 |

* Of course, you never see it again!

You can often get extra pocket money:

– when you visit aunts, uncles, grans or grandads (but they make you give them a sloppy kiss first)

– at Christmas time (measly £1 gift tokens)

– on your birthday (but, guess what? – your mum makes you open a bank account so you don't spend it)

– from the Tooth Fairy (okay, you're eight, but it's still worth a try)

You never get pocket money from:

– great grandmas and grandads (you just get a sticky boiled sweet, covered in cobwebs)

– big brothers and sisters (they just pinch it without asking)

– neighbours (you won't get your ball back either!)

● ●

* Empty your drawers on to your bed and sort them. You may discover stuff that is still useful, and things that bring back warm memories.

* Sort out your books. Put your storybooks together on one shelf and any fact books on another shelf. If you have a lot of time and patience you could put

the books in alphabetical order. Start with an author whose first (or last) name begins with 'A'.

* Ask if you can have a small plot of soil to turn into a vegetable garden. Why not try growing lettuces, radishes and carrots from seed? You could also have a go at growing the world's tallest sunflower. You will need very green fingers to beat the world record which is over seven metres tall.

If you do not have a garden it is possible to grow mustard and cress from seeds. Place the seeds on a piece of wet kitchen towel, laid in a shallow dish. Keep the seeds well watered and they will begin to grow roots. The seedlings can then be planted into small yoghurt pots filled with soil. Plastic egg cartons make great seedling holders too.

If your garden is small, or if you don't have one, why not have a window box or a plastic tub? Good window box plants are: daffodils, tulips, crocuses and hyacinths.

* Make up your own comic strip character. Give this character some amazing adventures. If you think you have come up with a really good idea why not send it to your local newspaper? It could make you famous!

* Take a few sheets of white paper, a pen, dice and some buttons. Now have a go at inventing a new board game. Write out the rules and challenge someone to a game.

* Look at a photograph of yourself. Trace your face on to a piece of paper and give yourself a crazy hairstyle and then add some fantastic looking clothes. Fluorescent pens are great to use and give a colourful look to 'the new you'.

← old school photo

'the new you' →

* Go through your parents' record collection and listen to the music they enjoyed when they were young and trendy. You might even end up liking some of it. If you do, make a tape for yourself. Or you could make a tape of all the worst songs and terrorise your friends with it! Watch your parents' faces as they relive their younger days (and prepared to be bored stiff by Dad's stories).

* Make a scary 'DO NOT DISTURB' sign out of card. You can hang it on your bedroom door handle to tell everyone that you want a bit of peace and quiet.

* Write out a list of your favourite things. It could include favourite films, videos, books, friends, presents, holidays, stories, music, food, pets – the list is endless.

* Make a scrap book of your favourite pop star. Fill it with interviews, photographs and newspaper clippings. You could also write a letter asking for an autograph and send it to the star's fan club.

* Design a mobile to hang over your bed. Put two strips of card into an 'X' shape and glue them together. Then draw and cut out something interesting to hang from them, for example, the planets in the Solar System. Tape a piece of thread on to each cut out planet, and tie (or tape) the threads on to the strips.

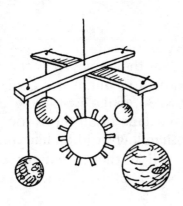

* Borrow a tape recorder, put on some music and have a go at karaoke. Make sure you keep the bedroom door closed to keep out your fans.

* Enter every competition you can think of. You can find them on the back of cereal packets and in the 'junk mail' that lands on your doormat. Since a lot of shops now run colouring competitions why not collect as many entry forms as you can find, colour them in and send them off. You might even win!

* Write a letter to a relative you have never met before. It will make their day and you could one day end up going somewhere exotic, like Australia or Skegness.

FAVOURITE

GAMES OF
EIGHT-YEAR-OLDS

ON THE RIVER

All you need: a line marked on the playground plus a few friends.

One player is the leader. The leader faces all the other players who must stand on the line at the start of the game.

The leader has three commands
– 'On the river'
– 'On the bank'
– 'In the mountains'

Whenever the leader says 'On the river' the players must jump on to the line.

Whenever the leader says 'On the bank' the players must jump in front of the line.

Whenever the leader says 'In the mountains' the players must jump behind the line.

Players must keep their feet together when they jump, or they are out. You are also out if you are the

last one to obey the leader's command. If you jump forwards when you should be jumping backwards you are also out.

The leader can say the commands in any order, and should try to fool the players by speaking quickly, or by repeating a command over again.

Variation: The game can be made harder if the leader uses these commands instead:
– 'Pineapples'
– 'Apples'
– 'Pinetrees'

SLEEPING LIONS
● ●

All you need: dry ground and a few friends

Choose a player to be the Mouse. The rest of the players lie down on the ground, with their eyes open, and pretend to be Sleeping Lions. The Mouse sneaks around trying to get the Lions to move. Any Lions caught moving are out. The Mouse is not allowed to touch the Lions. Instead it can blow raspberries, stare hard, or pull faces.

Lions are not allowed to cover their faces up, make any noise at all, or have their eyes closed. They can, however, breathe and blink!

When a Lion is out it becomes a Mouse. The game is over when there is only one Lion left.

TROLLS

• •

All you need: a playground area and, you guessed it, some friends

Choose a player to be the leader. Line up behind this person. Be ready to copy every move the leader makes.

To start the game the leader must transform into a Troll. Everyone in the line should copy the face and movements of this Troll. The leader then goes around the playground leaping, twisting and making hideous Troll–like noises.

At any time during the game the leader can turn into another Troll shape. Each Troll should be different from the one before. Try making them hop, stagger, or even crawl.

Variation: You could play a game where the leader changes from one wild animal into another.

THUNDER AND LIGHTNING

●●●●●●●●●●●●●●●●●●●●●●●●●●●●●

All you need: six or more friends

You are the leader so get your friends to form a circle and sit down. They must copy everything you do.

1) Tap your fingers lightly on your legs.

2) Pat your legs with your hands, and slowly make the sound become louder and louder.

3) Rub the palms of your hands together, so it sounds like wind. The quicker you do this the windier it sounds. Start to whistle.

4) Clap your hands together, making loud 'crashes'.

5) Make Thunder by stomping your feet on the ground.

The more friends you get to play this, the more realistic it will sound!

BUZZ

● ●

All you need: three friends, a blindfold

One blindfolded player is turned around a few times. This player has to try and catch the other players – who run about making 'buzzing' bee sounds.

The player wearing a blindfold must catch a buzzing player and guess the name of this person. Buzzers can make it harder by disguising their voices.

When the blindfolded player correctly guesses a buzzer's name the player who is caught has to put on the blindfold.

BAD EGGS!

● ●

All you need: a small ball (and larger friends)

The person who is 'on' holds a bad egg (the ball) and starts chasing everyone else. The others run away. When 'Bad eggs!' is shouted out by the 'on' player, everyone must stop completely still.

The player with the bad egg can take three paces towards someone and throw the egg at them. If the egg scores a direct hit then the splattered player becomes the person who is 'on'.

Extra rule:
When an egg is coming towards you, you are allowed to twist out of the way or duck, as long as your feet don't move.

TIME BOMB

All you need: a large ball and quite a few friends

Players form a circle. They begin by passing the ball clockwise to the next person along.

As soon as the ball is dropped, players begin a countdown – going 10...9...8...7...6...5...4...3...2...1... BOOM! During this countdown players are allowed to throw the ball quickly around, or across, the circle.

Whoever holds the ball, or is nearest to the ball, when players say BOOM! is 'out'. That player sits down and the game continues until there is only one person left standing up.

Extra rules:
The ball must always be kept moving during a countdown. Any players deliberately holding on to the ball before passing it are 'out'.

You must always make a proper attempt to get the ball if it is thrown to you. If you do not then you are also 'out'.

TODAY I WENT TO SCHOOL ...

All you need: a friend

Start the game off by saying, 'Today I went to school and did art.' Your friend then repeats this sentence and adds to it something done at school beginning with 'B':
    'Today I went to school and did art and basketball ...'
    You then add something that starts with 'C'.

Carry on adding to the sentence until one of you forgets something or hesitates. See if you can get all the way through the alphabet to 'Z'.

SAUSAGES

● ●

All you need: a friend

Find a quiet place where you're not likely to be hit by an Unidentified Flying Object. You have to ask your friend ten questions on whatever subjects you like. Your friend has to answer all the questions with the word 'Sausages'.

You might set questions like, 'What is your teacher's name?' or 'When you got up this morning, what did you find in the cereal packet?'.

You win if your friend smiles or laughs at any time during the game. You lose if this friend manages to keep a straight face.

DROODLES

● ●

All you need: a pen, paper and at least one friend

One person draws a wiggly line on the paper. The other player(s) has two minutes to turn the line into something recognisable, like a face or a mountain range.

Variation:
Get one person to draw a shape, such as a square. The other players have three minutes to make as many different objects as they can out of that shape.

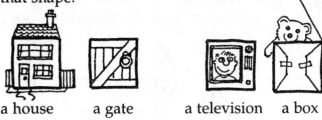

a house   a gate   a television   a box

SQUARES

All you need: paper, two coloured pens and a friend

Cover the paper with rows of dots (see the example below).

You start by drawing a line between two dots. Your friend should do the same. Continue the game until a square is made.

Whenever players make a square they put the first letter of their name inside it. Keep playing the game until all the dots have been used up.

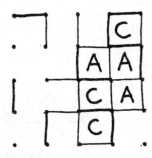

The player who made the most squares is the winner!

Variation:
Try the same game, but use triangles instead of squares. You must draw your dots like this:

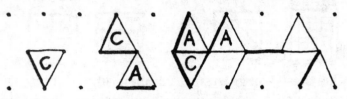

BOOKWORM

All you need: pencil, paper and some imagination

Some words are made up of two words:
bookworm = book + worm

In this game you must draw the longer word in a crazy way – using the smaller words as your guide. Then get a friend to guess the word you have drawn.

Here are some examples:

pancake (pan + cake)

122

carpet (car + pet)

Use these words to start yourself off:

treehouse	penknife	bookcase	handbag
moneybox	hatpin	hotdog	sunbed
eyedrops	beanbag	foxglove	armpit

TELEPHONES
● ●

All you need: a friend, a pad of paper and a pencil

Sit opposite your friend, and imagine you are both holding mobile phones. Dial your friend's number (make it up as you go along) and pass on a message.

While you are speaking, your friend must write down the message. When you have finished sending the message get your friend to read it back.

How well did your friend do? Decide if there was anything important missed out.

Here are some messages you might like to pass on. Pad them out with interesting details:

* It is your birthday and you want your friend to come to your house. Give clear directions on how to get there.

* You want your friend to make you a cake. Describe what it should look like, and get your friend to make a list of the ingredients.

Why not make up some of your own messages?

MIME TIME
●●●●●●●●●●●●●●●●●●●●●●●●●●●●●●

All you need: pencil, paper and a group of friends

Tear the paper into small strips. On each strip you should write out a task for someone to do. Here are some ideas:

* Get a left-handed friend to pick up a pencil.

* Ask a boy with black shoes to untie his laces.

* Get someone to tell you the time.

* Make all your friends hold hands and whistle.

Put all the pieces of paper face down on a table. Ask a friend to take a strip and read (silently) the words you have written. Your friend now has to get someone to do the task. No words are allowed. Only gestures, such as hand movements and nods, can be used. Give your friend a time limit of five minutes!

ONCE UPON ...

●●●●●●●●●●●●●●●●●●●●●●●●●●●

All you need: a friend

In this game you have to make up a story with your friend by building it up word by word.

You start by saying 'Once'. Your friend should say 'Upon'.

Then you carry on the story by making up the next word.

Now keep taking it in turns to add a new word.

WORDS IN WORDS

●●●●●●●●●●●●●●●●●●●●●●●●●●●

All you need: pencil, paper and a friend

Choose one of the words from these lists:

together	bananas	gingerbread
bunkbed	battered	windowpane
delivered	smothering	yellowed
smoothing	considering	greatest
discolour	rectangles	basketballs

See how many shorter words you can make out of the word you have chosen eg:

flickering = flick lick in ring

WHERE IN THE WORLD?

●●●●●●●●●●●●●●●●●●●●●●●●●●●●●●●

All you need: a friend

Start off by pretending to be somewhere in the world.

Your friend is allowed to ask you twenty questions such as 'Can you see Polar Bears?' or 'Do the people there wear clogs?'

You must only answer with a 'Yes' or a 'No'. You win if your friend cannot guess the correct place within twenty questions.

AND FINALLY: THINGS YOU HAVE DONE WHILE YOU'RE EIGHT

●●●●●●●●●●●●●●●●●●●●●●●●●●●●●

Here's a terrific tick list for you to fill in when you feel like it! (Or it's raining and there's nothing better to do.)

Whenever you do one of the things on the list give the box next to it a tick and scribble in the date! And when you've ticked them all off – then you're ready to be nine!

* I learned all the times tables off by heart. ☐

* I swam at least ten metres. ☐

* I have looked after a pet. ☐

* I stayed over at a friend's house. ☐

* I rode a two-wheeler bike for a minute without falling off. ☐

* I have been in a school play. ☐

* I appeared on television ☐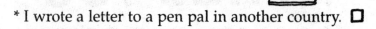

* I wrote a letter to a pen pal in another country. ☐

* I gave some money to charity. ☐

* I washed my own hair. ☐

* I started a hobby. ☐
  (My new hobby is ....)

* I made my parents breakfast in bed. ☐

* I began to play a musical instrument.
(I play the ....) ☐

* I have learned a great poem off by heart. ☐

* I have read a newspaper or magazine from cover to cover. ☐

* I can speak to someone in another language. ☐

* I have borrowed books from a library. ☐

* I have had a rotten illness like chicken pox. ☐

If you like, you can list all the other 'fab firsts' you have done while you're eight:

*

*

*

*

*

*